DEPARTMENT OF THE NAVY
HEADQUARTERS UNITED STATES MARINE CORPS
2 NAVY ANNEX
WASHINGTON, DC 20380-1775

I0440909

LIMITED DUTY OFFICER (LDO) AND WARRANT OFFICER (WO) PROGRAMS

DEPARTMENT OF THE NAVY
HEADQUARTERS UNITED STATES MARINE CORPS
2 NAVY ANNEX
WASHINGTON, DC 20380-1775

MCO 1040.42A
MCRC OE
3 May 00

MARINE CORPS ORDER 1040.42A

From: Commandant of the Marine Corps
To: Distribution List

Subj: LIMITED DUTY OFFICER (LDO) AND WARRANT OFFICER (WO)
       PROGRAMS

Ref: (a) SECNAVINST 1120.11A
       (b) MCO P1070.12J
       (c) ManMed, Chap. 15 (NOTAL)

Encl: (1) LDO Program
       (2) WO (Reserve) Program
       (3) WO (Regular) Program
       (4) WO (Gunner) Program
       (5) WO (Recruiter) Program
       (6) Procedures to Delay/Remove Appointment

1. Purpose. To provide administrative guidance in the
application/appointment process for the LDO and WO programs
per reference (a).

2. Cancellation. MCO 1040.42.

3. Summary of Revision. This order updates the application
format to include submission of tattoo photographs and Service
Record Book (SRB) page 11 entry regarding fraternization. In
addition, the format for delay/removal of appointment procedures
has been included as enclosure (6). There are other minor
administrative changes throughout the order.

4. Information

    a. Selection boards convene annually at Headquarters Marine
Corps to select qualified warrant officers for appointment to LDO
and Regular and Reserve enlisted Marines for appointment to the
grade of warrant officer (WO).

    b. Detailed administrative instructions concerning the LDO
and WO programs are contained in enclosures (1) through (6).
Selections for these programs will be accomplished annually based
on quotas by MOS. Marine Corps bulletins in the 1040 series will
be published annually to solicit applications for the subject
programs.

**DISTRIBUTION STATEMENT A: Approved for public release;
distribution is unlimited.**

c. Reference (a) establishes the policies, eligibility requirements, and board procedures for the subject programs. This order provides the sample applications required to apply for the subject programs and procedures to delay appointments and remove names from the selection list. This order is intended to be used for administrative purposes only.

5. Action. Commanding officers:

a. Review, endorse, and submit applications for appointment under the provisions of reference (a), enclosures (1) through (5), and Marine Corps bulletins in the 1040 series.

b. Review and submit recommendations for delay/removal of appointment per reference (a) and enclosure (6).

c. Ensure all enlisted Marines and warrant officers under their respective cognizance are familiar with reference (a).

6. Reserve Applicability. This order is applicable to the Marine Corps Reserve.

GARRY L. PARKS
By direction

DISTRIBUTION: PCN 10200281300

Copy to: 7000110 (55)
         7000124 (50)
         7000062 (25)
         7000120 (3)
         8145005 (2)
         7000099, 144/8145001 (1)

<u>LDO PROGRAM</u>

1. <u>Application Checklist</u>. Applications must contain the
following enclosures, if applicable:

    a. <u>Data Sheet</u>. List the data sheet in this enclosure as
enclosure (1) on the application.

    b. Certified copy of most recent <u>NAVMC 763, Appointment
Acceptance and Record</u>.

    c. Certified copy of <u>NAVMC 118 (13), Record of Conviction
by Court-Martial, of the Officer Qualification Record (OQR)</u>.
Only submit this enclosure if it is applicable.

    d. Certified copy of <u>NAVMC 118 (12), Offenses and
Punishments, OQR</u>. Only submit this enclosure if it is
applicable.

    e. Certified copy of all entries on <u>NAVMC 118 (11),
Administrative Remarks, OQR</u>. This enclosure is required in all
applications.

    f. Certified copy of all entries on <u>NAVMC 118 (3),
Chronological Record, OQR</u>. This enclosure is required in all
applications.

    g. <u>Basic Individual Record (BIR)</u>.

    h. <u>Basic Training Record (BTR)</u>.

    i. <u>Education Record (EDU)</u> of the Marine Corps Total Force
System (MCTFS).

    j. College transcripts and evidence of degree (if
available).

    k. Recent photograph per reference (b).

    l. <u>Transmittal of Service Records/Pay Documents (NAVMC 941)</u>
or similar transmittal form with self-addressed envelope. This
return receipt is used solely as an aid to verify that the
applications arrived at CMC (MMOA-3) and to preclude numerous
telephone calls verifying receipt.

ENCLOSURE (1)

1

(1) The transmittal must be properly addressed to the command to facilitate return. Type command address with all capital letters, no punctuation, centered on envelope. Return address must be left blank. Improperly addressed transmittals annot be readily returned.

(2) Commanding officers may initiate tracer action if not in receipt of an acknowledged transmittal within 30 days after deadline.

2. <u>Sample Application Format</u>. Applicants for the LDO program must use the format shown in Appendix A.

3. <u>Sample First Endorsement</u>. Applications must be forwarded for endorsement through the same chain of command as fitness reports and other special requests. The commanding officer must prepare the first endorsement using the format shown in Appendix B.

4. <u>Data Sheet</u>

a. The data sheet shown in Appendix C will be used for application processing and computer input only. Provide only the information requested.

b. The data sheet can be locally reproduced or typed as an original. If an original is typed, the entire data sheet which includes both the applicant's information and the checklist section must be typed in all capital letters, no punctuation, using a courier or courier new font, 12 pitch, letter quality print. The HQMC action checklist must be included at the bottom of the data sheet for review purposes by HQMC.

ENCLOSURE (1)

APPENDIX A
SAMPLE APPLICATION FOR LDO PROGRAM

SSIC
DATE

From: CWO2 John J. Doe, Jr. 000 00 0000/0000 USMC
To: Commandant of the Marine Corps (MMOA-3)
       3280 Russell Road, Quantico, VA 22134-5103
Via: (1) Immediate Commanding Officer
       (2) Endorsing chain of command

Subj: REQUEST FOR APPOINTMENT UNDER THE FISCAL YEAR 20XX
       LIMITED DUTY OFFICER (LDO) PROGRAM

Ref: (a) SECNAVINST 1120.11_
       (b) MCO 1040.42_
       (c) MCBul 1040 of (date)
       (d) MCO P1070.12_

Encl: (1) Data Sheet
       (2) NAVMC 763
       (3) OQR, page 12
       (4) OQR, page 11
       (5) BIR and BTR
       (6) OQR, page 3
       (7) College transcripts
       (8) Photograph
       (9) List any other enclosures as applicable

1. I am eligible (except for {type of waiver}) and apply for the
Fiscal Year 20XX Limited Duty Officer Program per references (a)
through (c). Enclosures (1) through (XX) are attached as requested.
The following information is submitted:

    a. Date of Birth: (YYMMDD)

    b. Present Pay Grade and Date of Rank: (W-?, YYMMDD)

    c. Off-duty courses completed or currently enrolled in
that are not shown in the MCTFS or on college transcripts:

    d. Military schools and correspondence courses completed or
currently enrolled in that are not shown in the MCTFS education
screens:

                                      Appendix A to
                                      ENCLOSURE (1)

e. Total amount of active naval service: (years, months, days) (If other than naval service is included in your Armed Forces Active Duty Base Date (AFADBD) on the BIR, show branch of service, periods of service, and highest grade held. Show all dates and times in year/month/day format. Compute all dates and times as of 1 June the year of the board.)

f. Amount of time as a warrant officer: (years/months/days)

g. MOSs for which applying: (Note: not all applicants will be qualified to apply for more than one MOS. Apply only for those MOSs in which qualified per the MOS Manual.)

(1) First Choice: 0000

(2) Second Choice: 0000

h. Years of actual experience and key billets held in first choice MOS.

i. Years of actual experience and key billets held in second choice MOS (if applicable).

j. A recent photograph is attached as enclosure (XX).

2. "I have a (type of security investigation) completed on (date)," or "I do not have an investigation completed but it was initiated on (date)."

3. "I, (Full Name), if selected for appointment to LDO and upon acceptance of such appointment, agree to remain on active duty for a period not less than 3 years, unless sooner separated for cause under the provisions of SECNAVINST 1920.6A, Administrative Separation of Officers. I understand that this obligation will run concurrently with any other legal obligation in force and will not serve to decrease any such obligation."

4. Show unit telephone number and point of contact. Indicate your administrative office's DSN and commercial numbers. Include electronic mail (e-mail) address if you can be reached via electronic messages.

SIGNATURE OF APPLICANT

Appendix A to
ENCLOSURE (1)

APPENDIX B
SAMPLE FIRST ENDORSEMENT FOR LDO PROGRAM

SSIC
Date

FIRST ENDORSEMENT on CWO2 John J. Doe 000 00 0000/0000 USMC
         application (originating code and date)

From: Commanding Officer
To: Commandant of the Marine Corps (MMOA-3)
Via: (Endorsing Chain of Command)

Subj: REQUEST FOR APPOINTMENT UNDER THE FISCAL YEAR 20XX
        LIMITED DUTY OFFICER (LDO) PROGRAM

Encl: (XX) Transmittal of Service Records/Pay Documents
             NAVMC 941

1. The information contained in the basic application and the
enclosures have been verified with the records on file at this
command and are correct. The applicant meets the basic
eligibility requirements (except for {type of waiver}) for the
Fiscal Year 20XX Limited Duty Officer Program.

2. The height and weight of the applicant is _____ inches and
_____ pounds. The applicant last took the PFT on (date) and
obtained the following score:

                Pull ups/Flex Arm Hang   20   (100)
                Crunches   100   (100)
                Run time   18:00   (100)
                Total   (300)

3. Enclosure (XX) is the completed Transmittal of Service
Record.

4. Commander's comments in the supporting justification will
specifically address the technical proficiency of the applicant
in the MOS for which applying and, where possible, cite the
accomplishments of the Marine in that field.

                                    Appendix B to
                                    ENCLOSURE (1)

5. Any recommendation must be fully justified by the commanding officer and must include one of the following recommendation categories:

    a. Recommended with enthusiasm.

    b. Recommended with confidence.

    c. Recommended with reservation.

    d. Not recommended.

6. In addition to the recommendation, any waiver requested must be fully justified by the commanding officer. (Omit this paragraph if it does not apply.)

7. If the endorsement is "Not recommended" or is otherwise derogatory or unfavorable, this paragraph must read: "The applicant has been counseled as to the nature and content of the endorsement per reference (d). The applicant has been given an opportunity to make a statement." Reference (d) provides further guidance. (Omit this paragraph if it does not apply.)

                    SIGNATURE OF COMMANDING OFFICER

APPENDIX C
DATA SHEET FOR LDO PROGRAM

COLUMN 1   COLUMN 2

A.   LAST NAME

B.   FIRST NAME

C.   MIDDLE INITIAL

D.   SSN

E.   PRESENT PAY GRADE

F.   PRESENT MOS

G.   MOS FOR WHICH APPLYING

H.   RACE/ETHNIC CODE (PER BIR)

I.   AGE (AS OF 1 JUN XX)

J.   ACTIVE NAVAL SERVICE
     (AS OF 1 JUN XX)

K.   AMT OF TIME AS A WO
     (AS OF 1 JUN XX)

==============HQMC==============ACTION==============ONLY==============
                              LDO PROGRAM

        CHECKLIST   WAIVERS
REQUIRED

_____   PHOTOGRAPH
_____   PAGE 12, OQR
_____   PAGE 11, OQR
_____   PAGE 3, OQR
_____   NAVMC 763

_____   BIR/BTR   ENDORSEMENTS
        _____   US CITIZEN
        _____   ANS 10 - 20   _____   RECOMMENDED
        _____   WO TIME > 8   _____   NOT RECOMMENDED

                              Appendix C to
                              ENCLOSURE (1)

WO (RESERVE) PROGRAM

1. <u>Application Checklist</u>. Applications must contain the following enclosures:

    a. <u>Data Sheet</u>. List the data sheet in this enclosure as enclosure (1) on the application.

    b. Certified copy of <u>NAVMC 118 (13), Record of Conviction by Court-Martial, of the Service Record Book (SRB)</u>. Submit this enclosure only if it is applicable.

    c. Certified copy of <u>NAVMC 118 (12), Offenses and Punishments, SRB</u>. This enclosure must be submitted even if there are no entries.

    d. Certified copy of all entries on <u>NAVMC 118 (11), Administrative Remarks, SRB</u>. This enclosure is required in all applications.

    e. <u>Certified copy of NAVMC 118 (9), Awards Page, SRB</u>.

    f. <u>Certified copy of NAVMC 118 (3), Chronological Record, SRB</u>.

    g. <u>Record of Service (ROS)</u>. The ROS is a computer generated screen from the MCTFS. The ROS shows PRO/CON marks for sergeants only. If the applicant has been a sergeant for more than three years, only average in service markings will be available.

    h. <u>Basic Individual Record (BIR)</u>.

    i. <u>Basic Training Record (BTR)</u>.

    j. <u>Education Record (EDU)</u>. The EDU is a computer-generated screen from MCTFS which shows all MCI courses and service schools completed. Submit this enclosure even if there are no courses completed.

    k. <u>Reserve Career Retirement Credit Record (RCRC)</u>. The RCRC is a computer generated screen from MCTFS (RT07) which shows the Reserve credit for retirement.

    l. College transcripts and evidence of degree (if available).

ENCLOSURE (2)

1

m. <u>Report of Medical Examination Standard Form 88 (SF88)</u> and <u>Report of Medical History Standard Form 93 (SF93)</u>. Due to past problems, Reserve applicants must be found physically qualified by the Bureau of Medicine and Surgery (BUMED) prior to consideration by the selection board. A current physical examination must include the SF88, SF93, and any supporting documents required to complete the physical per reference (c). Physical must be less than two years old as of the date of appointment to warrant officer. Commands must review the medical forms to ensure correctness and completion. Pay particular attention to the following items:

(1) Marks, tattoos, brands, and scars must be listed. Submit appropriate color photos of all tattoos and brands. Do not send photos of private areas.

(2) Dental records must include type and class. (Must be a Type I or II examination and must be a Class I or II qualification). Additionally, must be done by a dental officer and state acceptable or unacceptable.

(3) Date and result of current HIV Test must be listed in the "Other Tests" section of the SF88. "HIV drawn" or "results pending" statements are not acceptable. If results are available at the time of the preparation of the SF88, provide a certified copy of the Chronological Record of HIV Testing or the Lab printout.

(4) Distant vision must be correctable to 20/20. If uncorrected vision is not 20/20, SF88 must contain the manifest refraction. The statement "by lenses" is not acceptable.

(5) SF88 must have the audiogram completed. If audiogram shows high frequency hearing loss, include a consultation from an ear, nose & throat (ENT) specialist with additional audiograms.

(6) On SF93, any affirmative answers must be explained by the physician in physicians summary section and all supporting documents submitted.

n. Recent photograph per reference (b).

o. <u>NAVMC 10476, Reserve Qualification Summary</u>.

ENCLOSURE (2)

   p. Transmittal of Service Records/Pay Documents (NAVMC 941)
or similar transmittal form with self-addressed envelope. This return
receipt is used solely as an aid to verify that the applications arrived
at MCRC (OE) and to preclude numerous telephone calls verifying receipt.

       (1) The transmittal must be properly addressed to the command
to facilitate return. Type command address with all capital letters, no
punctuation, centered on envelope. Return address must be left blank.
Improperly addressed transmittals cannot be readily returned.

       (2) Commanding officers may initiate tracer action if not in
receipt of an acknowledged transmittal within 30 days after deadline.

2. Sample Application Format. Applicants for the WO (Reserve) program
must use the format shown in Appendix A to enclosure (2).

3. Sample First Endorsement. Applications must be forwarded for
endorsement through the same chain of command as fitness reports and
other special requests. The commanding officer must prepare the first
endorsement using the format shown in Appendix B to enclosure (2).

4. Data Sheet

   a. The data sheet shown in Appendix C will be used for application
processing and computer input only. Provide only the information
requested.

   b. The data sheet may be locally reproduced or typed as an original.
If an original is typed, the entire data sheet which includes both the
applicant's information and the checklist section must be typed in all
capital letters, no punctuation, using a courier or courier new font, 12
pitch, letter quality print. The HQMC action checklist must be included
at the bottom of the data sheet for review purposes by MCRC (OE).

5. Service Record Book Entry

   a. The Marine Corps has had great success with "grow-our-own"
enlisted-to-officer programs. These successful programs give the
Marine Corps a broad-based, highly experienced officer corps. One
unintended consequence of this success, however, relates to
fraternization.

                                                      ENCLOSURE (2)
                              3

b. Navy Regulations, Chapter 11, General Regulations, Section 5 (Rights and Restrictions) par 1165 (Fraternization Prohibited) states, "Personal relationships between officer and enlisted members that are unduly familiar and that do not respect differences in grade or rank are prohibited. Such relationships are prejudicial to good order and discipline and violate longstanding traditions of the Naval service." Fraternization may be charged as an offense under the Uniform Code of Military Justice. The only exceptions are familial relationships, defined as marriages that occur prior to the date of commission or appointment and relationships between parents and children or between siblings.

c. To prevent fraternization or the appearance of fraternization, it is imperative that our enlisted Marines are briefed on the Marine Corps guidelines relating to fraternization. Therefore, commanders are required to ensure that each Marine applying for an enlisted to officer program reads and understands the Marine Corps policy on fraternization. Each Marine must sign the following SRB, page 11 entry and submit a certified true copy as part of the application:

"I have read and understand the Marine Corps policy on fraternization. I understand that, as a commissioned or warrant officer, I will be required to conduct myself as an officer with respect to all enlisted personnel, of any service, at all times. Specifically, I understand that I may have to make significant changes in my current personal relationships with other service members if I become an officer. I also understand that fraternization is an offense under the UCMJ, and that the prohibition of fraternization does not make an exception for preexisting relationships other than marriages that took place prior to my date of commission or appointment to warrant officer or other family relationships, such as that between parents and children or between siblings."

6. Tattoos, Brandings, piercings

a. The Marine Corps takes a conservative approach to personal appearance. Uniform regulations stress that personal appearance is to be conservative and commensurate with the high standards traditionally associated with the Marine Corps. No eccentricities in dress or appearance are permitted because they detract from uniformity and team identity.

b.   The Marine Corps uniform regulations prohibit tattoos or brands on the neck and the head. Additionally, any tattoo that is gang, racist, sexist, or drug related is prohibited. In other areas of the body, tattoos or brands that are prejudicial to good order, discipline, and morale, or are of a nature to bring discredit upon the Marine Corps, are also prohibited.

c.   tattoos, body piercing, and non-dental tooth crowns are identified as body art, and commanders are tasked with upholding current regulations regarding eccentric appearance.

(1)   Four criteria will be used to evaluate tattoos and brands to see if they comply with Marine Corps standards. These criteria are content, location, size, and effect of associating the Marine Corps and the Marine Corps uniform with the tattoo or brand.

(2)   In order for the selection board to evaluate the tattoos and brands, the Marine must provide appropriate color photos which clearly identifies the tattoo, or brand, along with a description detailing location, size, and number of tattoos. In cases where the tattoo is in a private area, a written description will suffice.

d.   Commanders must screen all tattoos to ensure they meet the above criteria. The commander must state in the first endorsement, "I have viewed the applicant's tattoos or brands (photos and/or description) attached as enclosure (xx) and they are within the Marine Corps standards per the Marine Corps Uniform Regulations."

ENCLOSURE (2)

APPENDIX A
SAMPLE APPLICATION FOR RESERVE WARRANT OFFICER PROGRAM

SSIC
DATE

From: Sergeant John J. Doe, Jr. 000 00 0000/0000 USMCR
To: Commandant of the Marine Corps
Via: (1) Immediate Commanding Officer
      (2) Endorsing chain of command
      (3) Commanding General, Marine Corps Recruiting Command
           Code (OE), 3280 Russell Road, Quantico, VA 22134-5103

Subj: REQUEST FOR APPOINTMENT UNDER THE FISCAL YEAR 20XX
      ENLISTED TO WARRANT OFFICER (RESERVE) PROGRAM

Ref: (a) SECNAVINST 1120.11_
      (b) MCO 1040.42_
      (c) MCBul 1040 of (date)
      (d) MCO P1070.12_
      (e) MCO 1001.52_

Encl: (1) Data Sheet
      (2) Physical
      (3) SRB, page 12
      (4) SRB, page 11
      (5) SRB, page 9
      (6) SRB, page 3
      (7) BIR and BTR
      (8) ROS, EDU, RT07
      (9) Reserve Qualification Summary
      (10) Photograph
      (11) List any other enclosures as applicable

1. I am eligible (except for {type of waiver}) and apply for the
Fiscal Year 20XX Enlisted to Warrant Officer (Reserve) Program per
references (a) through (c). Enclosures (1) through (XX) are attached
as requested. The following information is submitted:

    a. Date of Birth: (YYMMDD)

    b. Permanent Pay Grade and Date or Rank: (E-X, YYMMDD)

    c. Off-duty courses completed or currently enrolled in that are
not shown in the MCTFS or on college transcripts:

                                        Appendix A to
                                        ENCLOSURE (2)

d. Military schools and correspondence courses completed or currently enrolled in that are not shown in the MCTFS education screens:

e. Total amount of qualifying <u>naval</u> service: (years, months, days), (If other than naval service is included in the Pay Entry Base Date (PEBD) on the BIR, show branch of service, periods of service, and highest grade held. Show all dates and times in year, month, day format. Compute all dates and times as of 1 December the year of the board.)

f. Amount of service for retirement purposes: (years, months, days).

g. MOS and Billet for which applying: (Note: not all applicants will be qualified to apply for more than one MOS. Apply only for the MOS in which qualified per the MOS Manual. You can choose as many specific billets from the vacancy list, in a qualified MOS, where you are willing to attend drills.)

    (1) First Choice: 0000 - RUC 00000 CITY, STATE

    (2) Second Choice: 0000 - RUC 00000 CITY, STATE

    (3) "I am willing to accept any billet in the qualified MOS listed above."

(Note: Applicants are required to provide their own transportation to and from the Home Training Center for any of the above choices.)

h. ASVAB/AFCT EL test score and test date: XXX (YYMMDD)
(If using the Scholastic Aptitude Test (SAT) or American College Test (ACT) to qualify, include the SAT/ACT test report as an enclosure.)

i. A recent photograph, per reference (d), is attached as enclosure (10).

2. "I have a (type of security investigation) completed on (date), " or "I do not have an investigation completed but it was initiated on (date)."

3. "I, (Full Name), if selected for appointment to warrant officer and upon acceptance of such appointment, agree to remain in the Ready Reserve, in a drilling unit, for a period not less than three years, unless sooner separated for cause under the provisions of SECNAVINST 1920.6A, Administrative Separation of Officers. I understand that this obligation will run concurrently with any other legal obligation in force and will not serve to decrease any such obligation."

4. SMCR personnel must include the following paragraph:

"I understand that selection to the grade of warrant officer guarantees that I will fill a billet in a Selected Marine Corps Reserve unit for which I have chosen."

5. Per reference (e), Active Reserve (AR) personnel who apply for an SMCR billet must include the following paragraph:

"I understand, if I am selected for SMCR warrant officer, I will be released from my AR contract on the 1st day of the seventh month after accepting my appointment."

6. Show unit telephone number and point of contact. Indicate your administrative office's DSN and commercial numbers. In addition, list home and civilian business telephone numbers and e-mail address (if you can be reached online to complete or correct your application).

                    SIGNATURE OF APPLICANT

                                        Appendix A to
                                        ENCLOSURE (2)

APPENDIX B
SAMPLE FIRST ENDORSEMENT FOR RESERVE WARRANT OFFICER PROGRAM

SSIC

Date

FIRST ENDORSEMENT on Sergeant John J. Doe 000 00 0000/0000 USMCR
application (originating code and date)

From: Commanding Officer
To: Commandant of the Marine Corps
Via: (1) (Endorsing Chain of Command)
       (2) Commanding General, Marine Corps Recruiting Command
            Code (OE), 3280 Russell Road, Quantico, VA 22134-5103

Subj: REQUEST FOR APPOINTMENT UNDER THE FISCAL YEAR 20XX
       ENLISTED TO WARRANT OFFICER (RESERVE) PROGRAM

Encl: (xx) Transmittal of Service Records/Pay Documents
             NAVMC 941

1. The information contained in the basic application and the
enclosures has been verified with the records on file at this
command and are correct. The applicant meets the basic eligibility
requirements (except for {type of waiver}) for the Fiscal Year 20XX
Enlisted to Warrant Officer (Reserve) Program.

2. The height and weight of the applicant is _____inches and _____
pounds. The applicant last took the PFT on ___(date)___ and obtained
the following score:

             Pull ups/Flex Arm Hang   20   (100)
             Crunches   100   (100)
             Run time   18:00   (100)
             Total   (300)

3. Enclosure (xx) is the completed Transmittal of Service Record.

4. "I have viewed the applicant's tattoos or brands (photos and/or
description) attached as enclosure (xx) and they are within the Marine
Corps standards per the Marine Corps Uniform Regulations." (Omit this
paragraph if it does not apply.)

Appendix B to
ENCLOSURE (2)

B-1

5. Commander's comments in the supporting justification will specifically address the technical proficiency of the applicant in the MOS for which applying and, where possible, cite the accomplishments of the Marine in that field.

6. Any recommendation must be fully justified by the commanding officer and must include one of the following recommendation categories:

    a. Recommended with enthusiasm.

    b. Recommended with confidence.

    c. Recommended with reservation.

    d. Not recommended.

7. In addition to the recommendation, any waiver requested must be fully justified by the commanding officer. (Omit this paragraph if it does not apply.)

8. If the endorsement is "Not recommended" or is otherwise derogatory or unfavorable, this paragraph must read: "The applicant has been counseled as to the nature and content of the endorsement per reference (d). The applicant has been given an opportunity to make a statement." Reference (d) provides further guidance. (Omit this paragraph if it does not apply.)

_____
SIGNATURE OF COMMANDING OFFICER

Appendix B to
ENCLOSURE (2)

APPENDIX C
DATA SHEET FOR RESERVE WARRANT OFFICER PROGRAM

COLUMN 1   COLUMN 2

A.   LAST NAME

B.   FIRST NAME

C.   MIDDLE INITIAL

D.   SSN

E.   PRESENT PAY GRADE

F.   PRIMARY MOS

G.   FIRST CHOICE MOS FOR WHICH APPLYING

H.   RACE/ETHNIC CODE (PER BIR)

I.   AGE (AS OF 1 DEC XX)

J.   TOTAL NAVAL SERVICE
     (AS OF 1 DEC XX)

K.   EL/SAT/ACT TEST SCORE:
     (circle one)

L.   ACTIVE RESERVE (circle one)   Y / N

=============HQMC==============ACTION===============ONLY=============
                    WO(RES) PROGRAM

CHECKLIST   WAIVERS REQUIRED

_____   TATTOO PHOTOS
_____   PHYSICAL
_____   PHOTOGRAPH
_____   SRB PAGES (12,11,9,3)
_____   ROS (SGTS ONLY)
_____   EDU   MCC _____   RUC _____
_____   RT07

   BIR/BTR   ENDORSEMENTS
_____   US CITIZEN   _____   RECOMMENDED
_____   TIS 8 - 20   _____   NOT RECOMMENDED
_____   EL > 110
_____   NAC

                                          Appendix C to
                                          ENCLOSURE (2)

WO (REGULAR) PROGRAM

1. <u>Application Checklist</u>. Applications must contain the following enclosures:

    a. <u>Data Sheet</u>. List the data sheet in this enclosure as enclosure (1) on the application.

    b. <u>Certified copy of NAVMC 118 (13), Record of Conviction by Court-Martial, of the Service Record Book (SRB)</u>. Submit this enclosure only if it is applicable.

    c. Certified copy of <u>NAVMC 118 (12), Offenses and Punishments, SRB</u>. This enclosure must be submitted even if there are no entries.

    d. Certified copy of all entries on <u>NAVMC 118 (11), Administrative Remarks, SRB</u>. This enclosure is required in all applications.

    e. Certified copy of <u>NAVMC 118 (9), Awards Page, SRB</u>.

    f. Certified copy of <u>NAVMC 118 (3), Chronological Record, SRB</u>.

    g. <u>Record of Service (ROS)</u>. The ROS is a computer-generated screen from MCTFS. The ROS shows PRO/CON marks for sergeants only. If the applicant has been a sergeant for more than three years, only average in service markings will be available.

    h. <u>Basic Individual Record (BIR)</u>.

    i. <u>Basic Training Record (BTR)</u>.

    j. <u>Education Record (EDU)</u>. The EDU is a computer-generated screen from MCTFS which shows all MCI courses and service schools completed. Submit this enclosure even if there even no courses completed.

    k. College transcripts and evidence of degree (if available).

ENCLOSURE (3)

1. <u>Report of Medical Examination Standard Form 88 (SF88)</u> and <u>Report of Medical History Standard Form 93 (SF93)</u>. Due to the volume of applicants for the Regular Warrant Officer Selection Board, active duty applicants must be found physically qualified by the Bureau of Medicine and Surgery (BUMED) after the results of the selection board are published and prior to appointment to warrant officer. A current precommissioning physical examination must include the SF88, SF93, and any supporting documents required to complete the physical per reference (c). A physical must be less than two years old as of the date of appointment to warrant officer. Commands must review the medical forms to ensure correctness and completion. Pay particular attention to the following items:

    (1) Marks, tattoos, brands, and scars must be listed. Submit appropriate color photos of all tattoos and brands. Do not send photos of private areas.

    (2) Dental record must include type and class. (Must be a Type I or II examination and must be a Class I or II qualification. Additionally, must be done by a dental officer and state acceptable or unacceptable.

    (3) Date and result of current HIV Test must be listed in the "Other Tests" section of the SF88. "HIV drawn" or "results pending" statements are not acceptable. If results are available at the time of the preparation of the SF88, provide a certified copy of the Chronological Record of HIV Testing or the Lab printout.

    (4) Distant vision must be correctable to 20/20. If uncorrected vision is not 20/20, SF88 must contain the manifest refraction. The statement "by lenses" is not acceptable.

    (5) SF88 must have the audiogram completed. If audiogram shows high frequency hearing loss, include a consultation from an Ear, Nose & Throat (ENT) specialist with additional audiograms.

    (6) On SF93, any affirmative answers must be explained by the physician in physicians summary section and all supporting documents submitted.

   m. Recent photograph per reference (b).

ENCLOSURE (3)

n. Transmittal of Service Records/Pay Documents (NAVMC 941) or similar transmittal form with self-addressed envelope. This return receipt is used solely as an aid to verify that the applications arrived at MCRC (OE) and to preclude numerous telephone calls verifying receipt.

(1) The transmittal must be properly addressed to the command to facilitate return. Type command address with all capital letters, no punctuation, centered on envelope. Return address must be left blank. Improperly addressed transmittals cannot be readily returned.

(2) Commanding officers may initiate tracer action if not in receipt of an acknowledged transmittal within 30 days after deadline.

2. Sample Application Format. Applicants for the WO (Regular) program must use the format shown in Appendix A to this enclosure.

3. Sample First Endorsement. Applications must be forwarded for endorsement through the same chain of command as fitness reports and other special requests. The commanding officer must prepare the first endorsement using the format shown in Appendix B to this enclosure.

4. Data Sheet

a. The data sheet shown in Appendix C to this enclosure will be used for application processing and computer input only. Provide only the information requested.

b. The data sheet may be locally reproduced or typed as an original. If an original is typed, the entire data sheet which includes both the applicant's information and the checklist section must be typed in all capital letters, no punctuation, using a courier or courier new, 12 pitch, letter quality print. The HQMC action checklist must be included at the bottom of the data sheet for review purposes by MCRC (OE).

5. Service Record Book Entry

a. The Marine Corps has had great success with "grow-our-own" enlisted-to-officer programs. These successful programs give the Marine Corps a broad-based, highly experienced officer corps. One unintended consequence of this success, however, relates to fraternization.

ENCLOSURE (3)

b. Navy Regulations, Chapter 11, General Regulations, Section 5 (Rights and Restrictions) par 1165 (Fraternization Prohibited) states, "Personal relationships between officer and enlisted members that are unduly familiar and that do not respect differences in grade or rank are prohibited. Such relationships are prejudicial to good order and discipline and violate longstanding traditions of the Naval service." Fraternization may be charged as an offense under the Uniform Code of Military Justice. The only exceptions are familial relationships, defined as marriages that occur prior to the date of commission or appointment and relationships between parents and children or between siblings.

c. To prevent fraternization or the appearance of fraternization, it is imperative that our enlisted Marines are briefed on the Marine Corps guidelines relating to fraternization. Therefore, commanders are required to ensure that each Marine applying for an enlisted to officer program reads and understands the Marine Corps policy on fraternization. Each Marine must sign the following SRB, page 11 entry and submit a certified true copy as part of the application:

"I have read and understand the Marine Corps policy on fraternization. I understand that, as a commissioned or warrant officer, I will be required to conduct myself as an officer with respect to all enlisted personnel, of any service, at all times. Specifically, I understand that I may have to make significant changes in my current personal relationships with other service members if I become an officer. I also understand that fraternization is an offense under the UCMJ, and that the prohibition of fraternization does not make an exception for preexisting relationships other than marriages that took place prior to my date of commission or appointment to warrant officer or other family relationships, such as that between parents and children or between siblings."

6. Tattoos, Brandings, piercings

a. The Marine Corps takes a conservative approach to personal appearance. Uniform regulations stress that personal appearance is to be conservative and commensurate with the high standards traditionally associated with the Marine Corps. No eccentricities in dress or appearance are permitted because they detract from uniformity and team identity.

ENCLOSURE (3)

4

b. the marine Corps uniform regulations prohibit tattoos or brands on the neck and the head. Additionally, any tattoo that is gang, racist, sexist, or drug related is prohibited. In other areas of the body, tattoos or brands that are prejudicial to good order, discipline, and morale, or are of a nature to bring discredit upon the Marine Corps, are also prohibited.

c. tattoos, body piercing, and non-dental tooth crowns are identified as body art, and commanders are tasked with upholding current regulations regarding eccentric appearance.

    (1) Four criteria will be used to evaluate tattoos and brands to see if they comply with marine Corps standards. These criteria are content, location, size, and effect of associating the Marine Corps and the Marine Corps uniform with the tattoo or brand.

    (2) In order for the selection board to evaluate the tattoos and brands, the Marine must provide appropriate color photos which clearly identifies the tattoo, or brand, along with a description detailing location, size, and number of tattoos. In cases where the tattoo is in a private area, a written description will suffice.

d. Commanders must screen all tattoos to ensure they meet the above criteria. The commander must state in the first endorsement, "I have viewed the applicant's tattoos or brands (photos and/or description) attached as enclosure (xx) and they are within the Marine Corps standards per the Marine Corps Uniform Regulations."

ENCLOSURE (3)

APPENDIX A
SAMPLE APPLICATION FOR REGULAR WARRANT OFFICER PROGRAM

SSIC
DATE

From: Sergeant John J. Doe, Jr. 000 00 0000/0000 USMC
To: Commandant of the Marine Corps
Via: (1) Immediate Commanding Officer
        (2) Endorsing chain of command
        (3) Commanding General, Marine Corps Recruiting Command
             Code (OE), 3280 Russell Road, Quantico, VA 22134-5103

Subj: REQUEST FOR APPOINTMENT UNDER THE FISCAL YEAR 20XX
        ENLISTED TO WARRANT OFFICER (REGULAR) PROGRAM

Ref: (a) SECNAVINST 1120.11_
        (b) MCO 1040.42_
        (c) MCBul 1040 of (date)
        (d) MCO P1070.12_

Encl: (1) Data Sheet
        (2) SRB, page 12
        (3) SRB, page 11
        (4) SRB, page 9
        (5) SRB, page 3
        (6) BIR/BTR
        (7) ROS, EDU
        (8) Photograph
        (9) List any other enclosures as applicable

1. I am eligible (except for {type of waiver}) and apply for the
Fiscal Year 20XX Enlisted to Warrant Officer (Regular) Program per
references (a) through (c). Enclosures (1) through (XX) are attached
as requested. The following information is submitted:

    a. Date of Birth: (YYMMDD)

    b. Permanent Pay Grade and Date of Rank: (E-?, YYMMDD)

    c. Off-duty courses completed or currently enrolled in
that are not shown in the MCTFS or on the college transcripts:

    d. Military schools and correspondence courses completed or
currently enrolled in that are not shown in the MCTFS education
screens:

                                        Appendix A to
                                        ENCLOSURE (3)

  e. Total amount of active naval service: (years, months, days).
(If other than naval service is included in the Armed Forces Active
Duty Base Date (AFADBD) on the BIR, show branch of service, periods
of service, and highest grade held. Show all dates and times in year,
month, day format. Compute all dates and times as of 1 February the
year of the appointment.)

  f. Amount of commissioned time (if a former officer):

  g. MOS for which applying: (Note: not all applicants will be
qualified to apply for more than one MOS. Apply only for the MOS in
which qualified per the MOS Manual.)

   (1) First Choice: 0000

   (2) Second Choice: 0000

   (3) "I am willing to accept any MOS in which the board
considers me qualified."

  h. ASVAB/AFCT EL test score and test date: XXX (YYMMDD)
(If using the Scholastic Aptitude Test (SAT) or American College
test (ACT) to qualify, include the SAT/ACT test report as an
enclosure.)

  i. A recent photograph, per reference (d), is attached as
enclosure (XX).

2. "I have a (type of security investigation) completed on (date),
" or "I do not have an investigation completed but it was initiated
on (date)."

3. "I, (Full Name), if selected for appointment to warrant officer and
upon acceptance of such appointment, agree to remain on active duty for
a period not less than three years, unless sooner separated for cause
under the provisions of SECNAVINST 1920.6A, Administrative Separation of
Officers. I understand that this obligation will run concurrently with
any other legal obligation in force and will not serve to decrease any
such obligation."

4. Show unit telephone number and point of contact. Indicate
your administrative office's DSN and commercial numbers. List e-mail
address if you can be reached online to complete or correct your
application.

SIGNATURE OF APPLICANT

Appendix A to
ENCLOSURE (3)

APPENDIX B
SAMPLE FIRST ENDORSEMENT FOR REGULAR WARRANT OFFICER PROGRAM

SSIC
Date

FIRST ENDORSEMENT on Sergeant John J. Doe 000 00 0000/0000 USMC
application (originating code and date)

From: Commanding Officer
To: Commandant of the Marine Corps
Via: (1)   Endorsing Chain of Command
        (2)   Commanding General, Marine Corps Recruiting Command
              Code (OE), 3280 Russell Road, Quantico, VA 22134-5103

Subj: REQUEST FOR APPOINTMENT UNDER THE FISCAL YEAR 20XX
        ENLISTED TO WARRANT OFFICER (REGULAR) PROGRAM

Encl: (XX) Transmittal of Service Records/Pay Documents
             NAVMC 941 (Rev 3-83)

1.   The information contained in the basic application and the
enclosures has been verified with the records on file at this command
and are correct.   The applicant meets the basic eligibility
requirements (except for {type of waiver}) for the Fiscal Year 20XX
Enlisted to Warrant Officer (Regular) Program.

2.   The height and weight of the applicant is _____ inches and _____
pounds.   The applicant last took the PFT on (date) and obtained the
following score:

        Pull ups/Flex Arm Hang   20   (100)
        Crunches   100   (100)
        Run time   18:00   (100)
        Total   (300)

3.   Enclosure (XX) is the completed Transmittal of Service Record.

4.   "I have viewed the applicant's tattoos or brands (photos and/or
description) attached as enclosure (xx) and they are within the Marine
Corps standards per the Marine Corps Uniform Regulations."   (Omit this
paragraph if it does not apply.)

Appendix B to
ENCLOSURE (3)

5. Any recommendation must be fully justified by the commanding officer and must include one of the following recommendation categories:

    a. Recommended with enthusiasm.

    b. Recommended with confidence.

    c. Recommended with reservation.

    d. Not recommended.

6. Commander's comments in the supporting justification will specifically address the technical proficiency of the applicant in the MOS for which applying, and where possible, cite the accomplishments of the Marine in that field.

7. In addition to the recommendation, any waiver requested must be fully justified by the commanding officer. (Omit this paragraph if it does not apply.)

8. If the endorsement is "Not recommended" or is otherwise derogatory or unfavorable, this paragraph must read: "The applicant has been counseled as to the nature and content of the endorsement per reference (d). The applicant has been given an opportunity to make a statement." Reference (d) provides further guidance. (Omit this paragraph if it does not apply.)

SIGNATURE OF COMMANDING OFFICER

Appendix B to
ENCLOSURE (3)

APPENDIX C
DATA SHEET FOR REGULAR WARRANT OFFICER PROGRAM

COLUMN 1   COLUMN 2

A. LAST NAME

B. FIRST NAME

C. MIDDLE INITIAL

D. SSN

E. PRESENT PAY GRADE

F. PRESENT MOS

G. FIRST CHOICE MOS FOR WHICH APPLYING

H. RACE/ETHNIC CODE (PER BIR)

I. AGE (AS OF 1 FEB XX)

J. ACTIVE NAVAL SERVICE (AS OF 1 FEB XX)

K. EL/SAT/ACT TEST SCORE:
    (Circle one)
===============HQMC===============ACTION=================ONLY============
                    WO(REG) PROGRAM

        CHECKLIST   WAIVERS REQUIRED

_____ TATTOO PHOTOS
_____ PHOTOGRAPH
_____ SRB PAGES (12,11,9,3)
_____ ROS (SGTS ONLY)
_____ EDU

        BIR/BTR   ENDORSEMENTS

_____ US CITIZEN   _____ RECOMMENDED
_____ ANS 8 - 20   _____ NOT RECOMMENDED
_____ EL > 110
_____ NAC

                                        MCC _____   RUC _____

                                            Appendix C to
                                            ENCLOSURE (3)

WO (GUNNER) PROGRAM

1. <u>Application Checklist</u>. Applications must contain the following enclosures:

a. <u>Data Sheet</u>. List the data sheet in this enclosure as enclosure (1) on the application.

b. Certified copy of <u>NAVMC 118 (13), Record of Conviction by Court-Martial</u>, of the Service Record Book (SRB). Submit this enclosure if it is applicable.

c. Certified copy of <u>NAVMC 118 (12), Offenses and Punishments</u>, SRB. This enclosure must be submitted even if there are no entries.

d. Certified copy of all entries on the <u>NAVMC 118 (11), Administrative Remarks, SRB</u>.

e. Certified copy of <u>NAVMC 118 (9), Awards Page, SRB</u>.

f. Certified copy of <u>NAVMC 118 (3), Chronological Record, SRB</u>.

g. <u>Basic Individual Record (BIR)</u>.

h. <u>Basic Training Record (BTR)</u>.

i. <u>Education Record (EDU)</u>. The EDU is a computer-generated screen from MCTFS which shows all MCI courses and service schools completed. Submit this enclosure even if there are no courses completed.

j. College transcripts and evidence of degree (if available).

k. Recent photograph per reference (b).

l. <u>Report of Medical Examination Standard Form 88 (SF88)</u> and <u>Report of Medical History Standard Form 93 (SF93)</u>. Applicants must be found physically qualified by the Bureau of Medicine and Surgery (BUMED) prior to appointment to warrant officer. A current precommissioning physical examination must include the SF88, SF93, and any supporting documents required to complete the physical per reference (c). A physical must be less than two years old as of the date of appointment to warrant officer. Commands must review the medical forms to ensure correctness and completion. Pay particular attention to the following items:

ENCLOSURE (4)

1

(1) Marks, tattoos, brands, and scars must be listed. Submit appropriate color photos of all tattoos and brands. Do not send photos of private areas.

(2) Dental record must include type and class. (Must be a Type I or II examination and must be a Class I or II qualification. Additionally, must be done by a dental officer and state acceptable or unacceptable.

(3) Date and result of current HIV Test must be listed in the "Other Tests" section of the SF88. "HIV drawn" or "results pending" statements are not acceptable. If results are not available at the time of the preparation of the SF88, provide a certified copy of the Chronological Record of HIV Testing or the Lab printout.

(4) Distant vision must be correctable to 20/20. If uncorrected vision is not 20/20, SF88 must contain the manifest refraction. The statement "by lenses" is not acceptable.

(5) SF88 must have the audiogram completed. If audiogram shows high frequency hearing loss, include a consultation from an Ear, Nose & Throat (ENT) Specialist with additional audiograms.

(6) On SF93, any affirmative answers must be explained by the physician in physicians summary section and all supporting documents submitted.

m. <u>Marine Gunner Essay</u>. Essay must be 200 - 400 words and must address the following subjects:

(1) The most compelling reason I desire to become a CWO (Marine Gunner) in the USMC.

(2) What I feel my duties will entail on a daily basis.

(3) How I intend to make the transformation to a warrant officer.

n. <u>NAVMC 941, Transmittal of Service Records/Pay Documents</u> or similar transmittal form with self-addressed envelope. This transmittal is used solely as an aid to verify that the applications arrived at MCRC (OE) and to preclude numerous telephone calls verifying receipt.

(1) The transmittal must be properly addressed to the command to facilitate return. Type command address with all capital letters, no punctuation, centered on envelope. Return address must be left blank. Improperly addressed transmittals cannot be readily returned.

(2) Commanding officers may initiate tracer action if not in receipt of an acknowledged transmittal within 30 days after deadline.

2. <u>Sample Application Format</u>. Applicants for the WO (Gunner) Program must use the format shown in Appendix A to Enclosure (4).

3. <u>Sample First Endorsement</u>. Applications must be forwarded for endorsement through the same chain of command as fitness reports and other special requests. The commanding officer must prepare the first endorsement using the format shown in Appendix B to Enclosure (4).

4. <u>Data Sheet</u>

    a. The data sheet shown in Appendix C will be used for application processing and computer input only. Provide only the information requested.

    b. The data sheet may be locally reproduced or typed as an original. If an original is typed, the entire data sheet which includes both the applicant's information and the HQMC checklist section must be typed in all capital letters, no punctuation, using a courier or courier new, 12 pitch, letter quality print. The HQMC checklist section must be included at the bottom of the data sheet for review purposes by HQMC.

5. <u>Service Record Book Entry</u>

    a. The Marine Corps has had great success with "grow-our-own" enlisted-to-officer programs. These successful programs give the Marine Corps a broad-based, highly experienced officer corps. One unintended consequence of this success, however, relates to fraternization.

    b. Navy Regulations, Chapter 11, General Regulations, Section 5 (Rights and Restrictions) par 1165 (Fraternization Prohibited) states, "Personal relationships between officer and enlisted members that are unduly familiar and that do not respect differences in grade or rank are prohibited. Such relationships are prejudicial to good order and discipline and violate longstanding traditions of the Naval service." Fraternization may be charged as an offense under the Uniform Code of Military Justice. The only exceptions are familial relationships, defined as marriages that occur prior to the date of commission or appointment and relationships between parents and children or between siblings.

c. To prevent fraternization or the appearance of fraternization, it is imperative that our enlisted Marines are briefed on the Marine Corps guidelines relating to fraternization. Therefore, commanders are required to ensure that each Marine applying for an enlisted to officer program reads and understands the Marine Corps policy on fraternization. Each Marine must sign the following SRB, page 11 entry and submit a certified true copy as part of the application:

"I have read and understand the Marine Corps policy on fraternization. I understand that, as a commissioned or warrant officer, I will be required to conduct myself as an officer with respect to all enlisted personnel, of any service, at all times. Specifically, I understand that I may have to make significant changes in my current personal relationships with other service members if I become an officer. I also understand that fraternization is an offense under the UCMJ, and that the prohibition of fraternization does not make an exception for preexisting relationships other than marriages that took place prior to my date of commission or appointment to warrant officer or other family relationships, such as that between parents and children or between siblings."

6. Tattoos, Brandings, piercings

a. The Marine Corps takes a conservative approach to personal appearance. Uniform regulations stress that personal appearance is to be conservative and commensurate with the high standards traditionally associated with the Marine Corps. No eccentricities in dress or appearance are permitted because they detract from uniformity and team identity.

b. The Marine Corps uniform regulations prohibit tattoos or brands on the neck and the head. Additionally, any tattoo that is gang, racist, sexist, or drug related is prohibited. In other areas of the body, tattoos or brands that are prejudicial to good order, discipline, and morale, or are of a nature to bring discredit upon the Marine Corps, are also prohibited.

ENCLOSURE (4)

c. tattoos, body piercing, and non-dental tooth crowns are identified as body art, and commanders are tasked with upholding current regulations regarding eccentric appearance.

(1) Four criteria will be used to evaluate tattoos and brands to see if they comply with Marine Corps standards. These criteria are content, location, size, and effect of associating the Marine Corps and the Marine Corps uniform with the tattoo or brand.

(2) In order for the selection board to evaluate the tattoos and brands, the Marine must provide appropriate color photos which clearly identifies the tattoo, or brand, along with a description detailing location, size, and number of tattoos. In cases where the tattoo is in a private area, a written description will suffice.

d. Commanders must screen all tattoos to ensure they meet the above criteria. The commander must state in the first endorsement, "I have viewed the applicant's tattoos or brands (photos and/or description) attached as enclosure (xx) and they are within the Marine Corps standards per the Marine Corps Uniform Regulations."

ENCLOSURE (4)

APPENDIX A
SAMPLE APPLICATION FOR WARRANT OFFICER (GUNNER) PROGRAM

SSIC
DATE

From: Gunnery Sergeant John J. Doe, Jr. 000 00 0000/0000 USMC
To: Commandant of the Marine Corps
Via: (1) Immediate Commanding Officer
       (2) Endorsing chain of command
       (3) Commanding General, Marine Corps Recruiting Command
            Code (OE), 3280 Russell Road, Quantico, VA 22134-5103

Subj: REQUEST FOR APPOINTMENT UNDER THE FISCAL YEAR 20XX
       ENLISTED TO WARRANT OFFICER (GUNNER) PROGRAM

Ref: (a) SECNAVINST 1120.11_
       (b) MCO 1040.42_
       (c) MCBul 1040 of (date)
       (d) MCO P1070.12_

Encl: (1) Data Sheet
       (2) SRB, page 12
       (3) SRB, page 11
       (4) SRB, page 9
       (5) SRB, page 3
       (6) BIR/BTR
       (7) EDU
       (8) Marine Gunner Essay
       (9) Photograph
       (10) List any other enclosures as applicable

1. I am eligible (except for {type of waiver}) and apply for the
Fiscal Year 20XX Enlisted to Warrant Officer (Gunner) Program per
references (a) through (c). Enclosures (1) through (XX) are attached
as requested. The following information is submitted:

    a. Date of Birth: (YYMMDD)

    b. Permanent Pay Grade and Date of Rank: (E-?, YYMMDD)

    c. Off-duty courses completed or currently enrolled in that are
not shown in the MCTFS or on college transcripts:

                              Appendix A to
                              ENCLOSURE (4)

A-1

   d. Military schools and correspondence courses completed or currently enrolled in that are not shown in the MCTFS education screens:

   e. Total Amount of active naval service: (years, months, days). (If other than naval service is included in the Armed Forces Active Duty Base Date (AFADBD) on the BIR, show branch of service, periods of service, and highest grade held. Show all dates and times in year, month, day format. Compute all dates and times as of 1 February the year of the appointment.)

   f. Amount of commissioned time (if a former officer):

   g. ASVAB/ACB-61 GT test score and test date: XXX (YYMMDD)

   h. Years of experience and key billets as an infantry platoon sergeant or equivalent infantry billet:

   i. A recent photograph, per reference (d), is attached as enclosure (XX).

2. "I have a (type of security investigation) completed on (date), " or "I do not an have investigation completed but it was initiated on (date)."

3. "I, (Full Name), if selected for appointment to warrant officer and upon acceptance of such appointment, agree to remain on active duty for a period not less than three years, unless sooner separated for cause under the provisions of SECNAVINST 1920.6A, Administrative Separation of Officers. I understand that this obligation will run concurrently with any other legal obligation in force and will not serve to decrease any such obligation."

4. Show unit telephone number and point of contact. Indicate your administrative office's DSN and commercial numbers. List e-mail address if you can be reached online to correct or complete your application.

                    SIGNATURE OF APPLICANT

APPENDIX B
SAMPLE FIRST ENDORSEMENT FOR WARRANT OFFICER (GUNNER) PROGRAM

SSIC
Date

FIRST ENDORSEMENT on GySgt John J. Doe 000 00 0000/0000 USMC
application (originating code and date)

From: Commanding Officer
To: Commandant of the Marine Corps
Via: (1) Endorsing Chain of Command
       (2) Commanding General, Marine Corps Recruiting Command
            Code (OE), 3280 Russell Road, Quantico, VA 22134-5103

Subj: REQUEST FOR APPOINTMENT UNDER THE FISCAL YEAR 20XX
       ENLISTED TO WARRANT OFFICER (GUNNER) PROGRAM

Encl: (XX) Transmittal of Service Records/Pay Documents
            NAVMC 941 (Rev 3-83)

1. The information contained in the basic application and the
enclosures has been verified with the records on file at this command
and are correct. The applicant meets the basic eligibility requirements
(except for {type of waiver}) for the Fiscal Year 20XX Enlisted to Warrant
Officer (Gunner) Program.

2. The height and weight of the applicant is _____ inches and _____
pounds. The applicant last took the PFT on (date) and obtained the
following score:

        Pull ups   20   (100)
        Crunches   100   (100)
        Run time   18:00   (100)
        Total   (300)

3. Enclosure (XX) is the completed Transmittal of Service Record.

4. "I have viewed the applicant's tattoos or brands (photos and/or
description) attached as enclosure (xx) and they are within the Marine
Corps standards per the Marine Corps Uniform Regulations." (Omit this
paragraph if it does not apply.)

                                        Appendix B to
                                        ENCLOSURE (4)

5. Any recommendation must be fully justified by the commanding officer and must include one of the following recommendation categories:

    a. Recommended with enthusiasm.

    b. Recommended with confidence.

    c. Recommended with reservation.

    d. Not recommended.

6. Commander's comments in the supporting justification with specifically address the technical proficiency of the applicant in MOS 0306, and where possible, cite the accomplishments of the Marine in that field.

7. In addition to the recommendation, any waiver requested must be fully justified by the commanding officer. (Omit this paragraph if it does not apply.)

8. If the endorsement is "Not recommended" or is otherwise derogatory or unfavorable, this paragraph must read: "The applicant has been counseled as to the nature and content of the endorsement per reference (d). The applicant has been given an opportunity to make a statement." Reference (d) provides further guidance. (Omit this paragraph if it does not apply.)

                _____
                SIGNATURE OF COMMANDING OFFICER

Appendix B to
ENCLOSURE (4)

APPENDIX C
DATA SHEET FOR WARRANT OFFICER (GUNNER) PROGRAM

COLUMN 1   COLUMN 2

A. LAST NAME

B. FIRST NAME

C. MIDDLE INITIAL

D. SSN

E. PRESENT PAY GRADE

F. PRESENT MOS

G. RACE/ETHNIC CODE (PER BIR)

H. AGE (AS OF 1 FEB XX)

I. ACTIVE NAVAL SERVICE
    (AS OF 1 FEB XX)

J. GT TEST SCORE:

=============HQMC=============ACTION==============ONLY=============
                    WO (GUNNER) PROGRAM

CHECKLIST   WAIVERS REQUIRED

_____ TATTOO PHOTOS
_____ PHOTOGRAPH
_____ ESSAY
_____ SRB PAGES (12,11,9,3)
_____ EDU

      BIR/BTR   ENDORSEMENTS

_____ US CITIZEN   _____ RECOMMENDED
_____ ANS 16 - 23   _____ NOT RECOMMENDED
_____ GT > 110
_____ NAC

                                    MCC _____ RUC _____

                                    Appendix C to
                                    ENCLOSURE (4)

WO (RECRUITER) PROGRAM

1. <u>Application Checklist</u>. Applications must contain the following enclosures:

    a. <u>Data Sheet</u>. List the data sheet in this enclosure as enclosure (1) on the application.

    b. Certified copy of <u>NAVMC 118 (13), Record of Conviction by Court-Martial</u>, of the Service Record Book (SRB). Submit this enclosure only if it is applicable.

    c. Certified copy of <u>NAVMC 118 (12), Offenses and Punishments</u>, SRB. This enclosure must be submitted even if there are no entries.

    d. Certified copy of all entries on <u>NAVMC 118 (11), Administrative Remarks, SRB</u>. This enclosure is required on all applicants.

    e. Certified copy of <u>NAVMC 118 (9), Awards Page</u>, SRB.

    f. Certified copy of <u>NAVMC 118 (3), Chronological Record, SRB</u>.

    g. <u>Record of Service (ROS)</u>. The ROS is a computer-generated screen from MCTFS. The ROS shows PRO/CON marks for sergeants only. If the applicant has been a sergeant for more than three years, only average in service markings will be available.

    h. <u>Basic Individual Record (BIR)</u>.

    i. <u>Basic Training Record (BTR)</u>.

    j. <u>Education Record (EDU)</u>. The EDU is a computer-generated screen from MCTFS which shows all MCI courses and service schools completed. Submit this enclosure even if there are no courses completed.

    k. College transcripts and evidence of degree (if available).

    l. <u>Report of Medical Examination Standard Form 88 (SF88)</u> and <u>Report of Medical History Standard Form 93 (SF93)</u>. Recruiter Warrant Officer Selection Board applicants must be found physically qualified by the Bureau of Medicine and Surgery (BUMED) prior to appointment to warrant officer. A current precommissioning physical examination must include the SF88, SF93, and any supporting documents required to complete the physical per reference (c).

A physical must be less than two years old as of the date of appointment to warrant officer. Commands must review the medical forms to ensure correctness and completion. Pay particular attention to the following items:

    (1) Marks, tattoos, brands, and scars must be listed. Submit appropriate color photos of all tattoos and brands. Do not send photos of private areas.

    (2) Dental record must include type and class. (Must be a Type I or II examination and must be a Class I or II qualification. Additionally, must be done by a dental officer and state acceptable or unacceptable.

    (3) Date and result of current HIV Test must be listed in the "Other Tests" section of the SF88. "HIV drawn" or "results pending" statements are not acceptable. If results are available at the time of the preparation of the SF88, provide a certified copy of the Chronological Record of HIV Testing or the Lab printout.

    (4) Distant vision must be correctable to 20/20. If uncorrected vision is not 20/20, SF88 must contain the manifest refraction. The statement "by lenses" is not acceptable.

    (5) SF88 must have the audiogram completed. If audiogram shows high frequency hearing loss, include a consultation from an Ear, Nose & Throat (ENT) specialist with additional audiograms.

    (6) On SF93, any affirmative answers must be explained by the physician in physicians summary section and all supporting documents submitted.

    m. Recent photograph per reference (b).

    o. <u>Transmittal of Service Records/Pay Documents (NAVMC 941)</u> or similar transmittal form with self-addressed envelope. This return receipt is used solely as an aid to verify that the applications arrived at MCRC (OE) and to preclude numerous telephone calls verifying receipt.

    (1) The transmittal must be properly addressed to the command to facilitate return. Type command address with all capital letters, no punctuation, centered on envelope. Return address must be left blank. Improperly addressed transmittals cannot be readily returned.

ENCLOSURE (5)

(2) Commanding officers may initiate tracer action if not in receipt of an acknowledged transmittal within 30 days after deadline.

2. <u>Sample Application Format</u>. Applicants for the WO (Recruiter) program must use the format shown in Appendix A to Enclosure (5).

3. <u>Sample First Endorsement</u>. Applications must be forwarded for endorsement through the same chain of command as fitness reports and other special requests. The commanding officer must prepare the first endorsement using the format shown in Appendix B to Enclosure (5).

4. <u>Data Sheet</u>

a. The data sheet shown in Appendix C to Enclosure (5) will be used for application processing and computer input only. Provide only the information requested.

b. The data sheet may be locally reproduced or typed as an original. If an original is typed, the entire data sheet which includes both the applicant's information and the checklist section must be typed in all capital letters, no punctuation, using a courier or courier new, 12 pitch, letter quality print. The HQMC action checklist must be included at the bottom of the data sheet for review purposes by MCRC (OE).

5. <u>Service Record Book Entry</u>

a. The Marine Corps has had great success with "grow-our-own" enlisted-to-officer programs. These successful programs give the Marine Corps a broad-based, highly experienced officer corps. One unintended consequence of this success, however, relates to fraternization.

b. Navy Regulations, Chapter 11, General Regulations, Section 5 (Rights and Restrictions) par 1165 (Fraternization Prohibited) states, "Personal relationships between officer and enlisted members that are unduly familiar and that do not respect differences in grade or rank are prohibited. Such relationships are prejudicial to good order and discipline and violate longstanding traditions of the Naval service." Fraternization may be charged as an offense under the Uniform Code of Military Justice. The only exceptions are familial relationships, defined as marriages that occur prior to the date of commission or appointment and relationships between parents and children or between siblings.

ENCLOSURE (5)

c. To prevent fraternization or the appearance of fraternization, it is imperative that our enlisted Marines are briefed on the Marine Corps guidelines relating to fraternization. Therefore, commanders are required to ensure that each Marine applying for an enlisted to officer program reads and understands the Marine Corps policy on fraternization. Each Marine must sign the following SRB, page 11 entry and submit a certified true copy as part of the application:

"I have read and understand the Marine Corps policy on fraternization. I understand that, as a commissioned or warrant officer, I will be required to conduct myself as an officer with respect to all enlisted personnel, of any service, at all times. Specifically, I understand that I may have to make significant changes in my current personal relationships with other service members if I become an officer. I also understand that fraternization is an offense under the UCMJ, and that the prohibition of fraternization does not make an exception for preexisting relationships other than marriages that took place prior to my date of commission or appointment to warrant officer or other family relationships, such as that between parents and children or between siblings."

6. Tattoos, Brandings, piercings

a. The Marine Corps takes a conservative approach to personal appearance. Uniform regulations stress that personal appearance is to be conservative and commensurate with the high standards traditionally associated with the Marine Corps. No eccentricities in dress or appearance are permitted because they detract from uniformity and team identity.

b. The Marine Corps uniform regulations prohibit tattoos or brands on the neck and the head. Additionally, any tattoo that is gang, racist, sexist, or drug related is prohibited. In other areas of the body, tattoos or brands that are prejudicial to good order, discipline, and morale, or are of a nature to bring discredit upon the Marine Corps, are also prohibited.

c. tattoos, body piercing, and non-dental tooth crowns are identified as body art, and commanders are tasked with upholding current regulations regarding eccentric appearance.

ENCLOSURE (5)

(1) Four criteria will be used to evaluate tattoos and brands to see if they comply with Marine Corps standards. These criteria are content, location, size, and effect of associating the Marine Corps and the Marine Corps uniform with the tattoo or brand.

(2) In order for the selection board to evaluate the tattoos and brands, the Marine must provide appropriate color photos which clearly identifies the tattoo, or brand, along with a description detailing location, size, and number of tattoos. In cases where the tattoo is in a private area, a written description will suffice.

    d. Commanders must screen all tattoos to ensure they meet the above criteria. The commander must state in the first endorsement, "I have viewed the applicant's tattoos or brands (photos and/or description) attached as enclosure (xx) and they are within the Marine Corps standards per the Marine Corps Uniform Regulations."

APPENDIX A

SAMPLE APPLICATION FOR RECRUITER WARRANT OFFICER PROGRAM

SSIC
DATE

From: Sergeant John J. Doe, Jr. 000 00 0000/0000 USMC
To: Commandant of the Marine Corps
Via: (1) Immediate Commanding Officer
      (2) Endorsing chain of command
      (3) Commanding General, Marine Corps Recruiting Command
           Code (OE), 3280 Russell Road, Quantico, VA 22134-5103

Subj: REQUEST FOR APPOINTMENT UNDER THE FISCAL YEAR 20XX
      ENLISTED TO WARRANT OFFICER (RECRUITER) PROGRAM

Ref: (a) SECNAVINST 1120.11_
      (b) MCO 1040.42_
      (c) MCBul 1040 of (date)
      (d) MCO P1070.12_

Encl: (1) Data Sheet
      (2) SRB, page 12
      (3) SRB, page 11
      (4) SRB, page 9
      (5) SRB, page 3
      (6) BIR/BTR
      (7) EDU
      (8) Photograph
      (9) List any other enclosures as applicable

1. I am eligible (except for {type of waiver}) and apply for the
Fiscal Year 20XX Enlisted to Warrant Officer (Recruiter) Program per
references (a) through (c). Enclosures (1) through (XX) are attached
as requested. The following information is submitted:

    a. Date of Birth: (YYMMDD)

    b. Permanent Pay Grade and Date of Rank: (E-?, YYMMDD)

    c. Off-duty courses completed or currently enrolled in that are
not shown in the MCTFS or on college transcripts:

                                        Appendix A to
                                        ENCLOSURE (5)

    d. Military schools and correspondence courses completed or currently enrolled in that are not shown in MCTFS education screens:

    e. Total amount of active naval service: (years, months, days). (If other than naval service is included in the Armed Forces Active Duty Base Date (AFADBD) on the BIR, show branch of service, periods of service, and highest grade held. Show all dates and times in year, month, day format. Compute all dates and times as of 1 February the year of the appointment.)

    f. Amount of commissioned time (if a former officer):

    g. ASVAB/AFCT EL test score and test date: XXX (YYMMDD) (If using the Scholastic Aptitude Test (SAT) or American College test (ACT) to qualify, include the SAT/ACT test report as an enclosure.)

    h. A recent photograph, per reference (d), is attached as enclosure (XX).

2. "I have a (type of security investigation) completed on (date)," or "I do not have an investigation completed but it was initiated on (date)."

3. "I, (Full Name), if selected for appointment to warrant officer and upon acceptance of such appointment, agree to remain on active duty for a period not less than three years, unless sooner separated for cause under the provisions of SECNAVINST 1920.6A, Administrative Separation of Officers. I understand that this obligation will run concurrently with any other legal obligation in force and will not serve to decrease any such obligation."

4. "I (Full Name), understand that officers do not receive Special Duty Assignment (SDA) pay and that if selected and upon appointment to warrant officer, my SDA pay will be discontinued."

5. Show unit telephone number and point of contact. Indicate your administrative office's DSN and commercial numbers. List e-mail address if you can be reached online to complete or correct your application.

SIGNATURE OF APPLICANT

Appendix A to
ENCLOSURE (5)

APPENDIX B
SAMPLE FIRST ENDORSEMENT FOR RECRUITER WARRANT OFFICER PROGRAM

SSIC
Date

FIRST ENDORSEMENT on Sergeant John J. Doe 000 00 0000/0000 USMC
application (originating code and date)

From: Commanding Officer
To: Commandant of the Marine Corps
Via: (1) Endorsing Chain of Command
       (2) Commanding General, Marine Corps Recruiting Command
            Code (OE), 3280 Russell Road, Quantico, VA 22134-5103

Subj: REQUEST FOR APPOINTMENT UNDER THE FISCAL YEAR 20XX
       ENLISTED TO WARRANT OFFICER (RECRUITER) PROGRAM

Encl: (XX) Transmittal of Service Records/Pay Documents
            NAVMC 941 (Rev 3-83)

1. The information contained in the basic application and the
enclosures has been verified with the records on file at this command
and are correct. The applicant meets the basic eligibility
requirements (except for {type of waiver}) for the Fiscal Year 20XX
Enlisted to Warrant Officer (Recruiter) Program.

2. The height and weight of the applicant is _____ inches and _____
pounds. The applicant last took the PFT on (date) and obtained the
following score:

        Pull ups/Flex Arm Hang   20   (100)
        Crunches   100   (100)
        Run time   18:00   (100)
        Total   (300)

3. Enclosure (XX) is the completed Transmittal of Service Record.

4. "I have viewed the applicant's tattoos or brands (photos and/or
description) attached as enclosure (xx) and they are within the
Marine Corps standards per the Marine Corps Uniform Regulations."
(Omit this paragraph if it does not apply.)

                                    Appendix B to
                                    ENCLOSURE (5)

5. Any recommendation must be fully justified by the commanding officer and must include one of the following recommendation categories:

    a. Recommended with enthusiasm.

    b. Recommended with confidence.

    c. Recommended with reservation.

    d. Not recommended.

6. Commander's comments in the supporting justification will specifically address the technical proficiency of the applicant in the Recruiting field, and where possible, cite the accomplishments of the Marine in that field.

7. In addition to the recommendation, any waiver requested must be fully justified by the commanding officer. (Omit this paragraph if it does not apply.)

8. If the endorsement is "Not recommended" or is otherwise derogatory or unfavorable, this paragraph must read: "The applicant has been counseled as to the nature and content of the endorsement per reference (d). The applicant has been given an opportunity to make a statement." Reference (d) provides further guidance. (Omit this paragraph if it does not apply.)

_____

SIGNATURE OF COMMANDING OFFICER

Appendix B to
ENCLOSURE (5)

APPENDIX C
DATA SHEET FOR RECRUITER WARRANT OFFICER PROGRAM

COLUMN 1   COLUMN 2

A. LAST NAME

B. FIRST NAME

C. MIDDLE INITIAL

D. SSN

E. PRESENT PAY GRADE

F. PRESENT MOS

G. MOS FOR WHICH APPLYING

H. RACE/ETHNIC CODE (PER BIR)

I. AGE (AS OF 1 FEB XX)

J. ACTIVE NAVAL SERVICE (AS OF 1 FEB XX)

K. EL/SAT/ACT TEST SCORE:
    (Circle one)
===============HQMC===============ACTION==================ONLY===========
                WO (RECRUITER) PROGRAM

      CHECKLIST   WAIVERS REQUIRED

_____ TATTOO PHOTOS
_____ PHOTOGRAPH
_____ SRB PAGES (12,11,9,3)
_____ EDU

      BIR/BTR   ENDORSEMENTS

_____ US CITIZEN   _____ RECOMMENDED
_____ ANS 8 - 20   _____ NOT RECOMMENDED
_____ 3 YRS as 8412
_____ EL > 110
_____ NAC

                                   MCC _____ RUC _____

                                          Appendix C to
                                          ENCLOSURE (5)

DELAY/REMOVAL OF APPOINTMENT PROCEDURES

1. The purpose of delaying an appointment is to provide a reasonable period of time to determine whether the name of that individual should be removed from the list approved by the Secretary of the Navy per reference (a).

2. The appointment of an individual may be delayed for the following reasons:

(1) An investigation is being conducted to determine whether disciplinary action of any kind should be brought against the individual.

(2) Sworn charges against the individual have been received by an officer exercising special courts-martial jurisdiction over the individual and such charges have not been disposed of.

(3) The individual is being processed for an administrative separation for cause.

(4) A criminal proceeding in a Federal or State court is pending against the individual.

(5) There is cause to believe that the individual does not meet the eligibility requirements per reference (a), except those which have been waived by CMC.

3. An appointment may not be delayed unless the individual has been given written notice of the grounds for the delay by the officer exercising special courts-martial jurisdiction over the individual or by CMC. The individual shall acknowledge receipt of such notification in writing. The individual shall be afforded an opportunity to submit a written statement to CMC concerning the delay. If the individual declines to make a statement, the individual must submit a statement to that effect. Appendix A to Enclosure (6) contains a sample notification letter to the individual being delayed, a sample acknowledgment of notification statement, and the recommendation to CMC to delay the appointment.

4. An appointment may not be delayed more than 90 days after final action has been taken by the appropriate authority.

ENCLOSURE (6)

5. The commander recommending the delay will be notified of the decision and provided further procedural guidance by CMC.

6. Upon completion of the basis for delay, if CMC determines that the individual's name should be removed from the selection list, the individual will be notified of such action and be afforded the opportunity to submit a written statement to the Secretary of the Navy via CMC. Follow the same guidance as in paragraph 3 above. Appendix B to this enclosure contains sample notification letter, acknowledgment of receipt, and recommendation for removal from the selection list.

7. The recommendation for removal, the individual's statement, and the remainder of the case file shall be forwarded to SECNAV for decision. The recommendation for removal must be submitted to SECNAV prior to the expiration of the time limit.

8. An individual whose appointment was delayed and is later determined to be qualified for appointment, may have the same date of rank and the same effective date for pay and allowances had no delay intervened.

SAMPLE NOTIFICATION OF DELAY

From: Commanding Officer
To: Sergeant John J. Doe, Jr. 000 00 0000/0000 USMC

Subj: NOTIFICATION OF REQUEST TO DELAY APPOINTMENT

Ref: (a) SecNavInst 1120.11_

Encl: (1) Acknowledgment of Notification

1. On _____DATE_____, the Secretary of the Navy approved the selection list for appointment to the grade of warrant officer.

2. Subsequent to the release of the selection results, (explain the basis for delay (i.e., pending investigation, civil charges, etc)). As a result and per the reference, your appointment to warrant officer is being delayed until all investigatory, administrative, or disciplinary proceedings are completed. At that time, a decision will be made as to what, if any, further action is necessary regarding your appointment.

3. You have the opportunity to make a statement concerning this matter. The enclosure is an acknowledgment of receipt. Please return this acknowledgment and any matters you wish to submit at this time, within 10 days of your receipt of this letter. The enclosure and any matters you wish to submit should be addressed, through your chain of command, to the Commandant of the Marine Corps via the Commanding General, Marine Corps Recruiting Command (OE), 3280 Russell Road, Quantico, VA 22134-5103.

_____
SIGNATURE OF COMMANDING OFFICER

Appendix A to
ENCLOSURE (6)

A-1

SAMPLE ACKNOWLEDGMENT OF NOTIFICATION

SSIC
DATE

From: Sergeant John J. Doe, Jr. 000 00 0000/0000 USMC
To: Commandant of the Marine Corps
Via: (1) Commanding Officer
        (2) Commanding General
        (3) Commanding General, Marine Corps Recruiting Command
             Code (OE), 3280 Russell Road, Quantico, VA 22134-5103

Subj: ACKNOWLEDGEMENT OF NOTIFICATION

Ref: (a) CO ltr 1040 of (date)

1. I acknowledge receipt of the reference notifying me of your
recommendation concerning my delay of appointment to warrant officer.

2. I understand I may submit a written statement to the Commandant of
the Marine Corps via the Commanding General, Marine Corps Recruiting
Command (OE).

3. I understand that all materials I desire to submit must be provided
within 10 days of the receipt of the reference.

4. ( ) I desire to submit a statement to the Commandant of the Marine
Corps.

    ( ) I do not desire to submit a statement at this time.

_____
SIGNATURE

Date Notified: _____

Appendix A to
ENCLOSURE (6)

A-2

SAMPLE REQUEST TO DELAY APPOINTMENT

SSIC
DATE

From: Commanding Officer
To: Commandant of the Marine Corps
Via: (1) Commanding General, (SNMs command)
       (2) Commanding General, Marine Corps Recruiting Command
            (Code OE), 3280 Russell Road, Quantico, VA 22134-5103

Subj: REQUEST TO DELAY APPOINTMENT TO WARRANT OFFICER ICO
       SERGEANT JOHN J. DOE, JR. 000 00 0000/0000 USMC

Ref: (a) SecNavInst 1120.11_

Encl: (1) CO,___ (SSIC) ltr of (DATE)
       (2) SNM's Acknowledgment of Notification

1. Per the reference, I recommend SNM's appointment to warrant officer
be delayed pending (BASIS FOR DELAY).

2. Background paragraph regarding basis for delay.

3. Sergeant Doe has been notified of the proposed action per enclosures
(1) and (2).

4. SNM has/has not submitted a statement on his behalf.

5. Point of contact and telephone number regarding this matter is:

_____   _____
SIGNATURE OF COMMANDING OFFICER

Appendix A to
ENCLOSURE (6)

A-3

SAMPLE NOTIFICATION OF REMOVAL FROM SELECTION LIST

                                                SSIC
                                                DATE

From: Commanding Officer
To: Sergeant John J. Doe, Jr. 000 00 0000/0000 USMC

Subj: NOTIFICATION OF REQUEST TO REMOVE YOUR NAME FROM
        FROM THE SELECTION LIST

Ref: (a) SecNavInst 1120.11_

Encl: (1) Acknowledgment of Notification

1. On _____DATE_____, the Commandant of the Marine Corps approved a
request to delay your appointment to warrant officer pending (basis
for delay).

2. As a result of (Basis for delay findings) and per the reference, I
am recommending the Secretary of the Navy remove your name from the
selection list.

3. You have the opportunity to make a statement concerning this matter
to the Secretary of the Navy. The enclosure is an acknowledgment of
receipt. Please return this acknowledgment and any matters you wish to
submit at this time, within 10 days of your receipt of this letter. The
enclosure and any matters you wish to submit should be addressed, through
your chain of command, to the Commandant of the Marine Corps via the
Commanding General, Marine Corps Recruiting Command (OE), 3280 Russell
Road, Quantico, VA 22134-5103.

                    _____
                    SIGNATURE OF COMMANDING OFFICER

                                        Appendix B to
                                        ENCLOSURE (6)

                            B-1

SAMPLE ACKNOWLEDGMENT OF NOTIFICATION

SSIC
DATE

From: Sergeant John J. Doe, Jr. 000 00 0000/0000 USMC
To: Secretary of the Navy
Via: (1) Commanding Officer
      (2) Commanding General (SNMs command)
      (3) Commanding General, Marine Corps Recruiting Command
      (4) Commandant of the Marine Corps

Subj: ACKNOWLEDGEMENT OF NOTIFICATION

Ref: (a) CO, ___ (SSIC) ltr of (date)

1. I acknowledge receipt of the reference notifying me of the
recommendation to remove my name from the selection list.

2. I understand I may submit a written statement to the Secretary of
the Navy via the Commandant of the Marine Corps.

3. I understand that all materials I desire to submit must be provided
within 10 days of the receipt of the reference.

4. ( ) I desire to submit a statement to the Secretary of the Navy.

    ( ) I do not desire to submit a statement at this time.

                         _____
                              SIGNATURE

Date Notified: _____

SAMPLE REQUEST FOR REMOVAL FROM THE SELECTION LIST

SSIC
DATE

From: Commanding Officer
To: Commandant of the Marine Corps
Via: (1) Commanding General (SNMs command)
       (2) Commanding General, Marine Corps Recruiting Command
            (Code OE), 3280 Russell Road, Quantico, VA 22134-5103

Subj: REMOVAL FROM THE FYXX _____ SELECTION LIST ICO
       SERGEANT JOHN J. DOE, JR. 000 00 0000/0000 USMC

Ref: (a) SecNavInst 1120.11_

Encl: (1) Results of (basis for delay)
       (2) CO,___ (SSIC) ltr of (DATE)
       (3) SNM's Acknowledgment of Notification

1. Per the reference, I recommend SNM's name be removed from the
subject selection list under the authority of reference (a).

2. Background paragraph regarding outcome of basis for delay.
Enclosure (1) contains the results of (basis for delay).

3. Sergeant Doe has been notified of the proposed action per
enclosures (1) and (2).

4. SNM has/has not submitted a statement on his behalf.

5. Point of contact and telephone number regarding this matter is:

                 _____
                 SIGNATURE OF COMMANDING OFFICER

                                    Appendix B to
                                    ENCLOSURE (6)